RESTLESS CONTINENT

Aja Couchois Duncan

RESTLESS CONTINENT

LITMUS PRESS | 2016

ISBN: 978-1-933959-30-6

Cover art: Erin Washington, "Sisyphus." Chalk and acrylic on panel. 40" x 50". 2014.

Design and Typesetting: HR Hegnauer

Litmus Press is a program of Ether Sea Projects, Inc., a 501(c)(3) non-profit literature and arts organization. Dedicated to supporting innovative, cross-genre writing, the press publishes the work of translators, poets, and other writers, and organizes public events in their support. We encourage interaction between poets and visual artists by featuring contemporary artworks on the covers of our books. By actualizing the potential linguistic, cultural, and political benefits of international literary exchange, we aim to ensure that our poetic communities remain open-minded and vital.

Litmus Press publications are made possible by the New York State Council on the Arts with support from Governor Andrew Cuomo and the New York State Legislature. Additional support for Litmus Press comes from the Leslie Scalapino – O Books Fund, individual members and donors. All contributions are fully tax-deductible.

Cataloging-in-publication data is available from the Library of Congress.

Litmus Press
925 Bergen Street, Suite 405
Brooklyn, New York 11238
litmuspress.org

Small Press Distribution
1341 Seventh Street
Berkeley, California 94710
spdbooks.org

Bring me the sun. Bear it on the palm of your hand...
Bring me the brains of the sky so I may see how large they are...
...bring me the girl with the watery teeth...

Fragrant shall be her odor when I remove her skirt...

LESLIE MARMON SILKO
Almanac of the Dead

We hold mirrors. Bloody our lip under the rent in the backdoor.
They crow for the quick and the dead and on the third day
they rise and crow again.

Very soon now we can return to our life of wonder and regret.

C.D. WRIGHT
Just Whistle

EMERGING FROM THE MUCK

if they say we have come from
oceanic witnesses
then who am i to differ

we who are land and battle
no longer remember
white caps, the pelagic suffering

say goodbye to the fog and smoke
this lingering sadness of lung
not say and want to mean it
even the tundra blossoms
seeds blanketed in ice
like you, a tiny frozen thing
the wind carves into days
makes a stab at the heart
this thrush
sea foam and asphalt

there is a silicon pouch where my heart used to be
i call her bitch to show her i don't miss her
she calls me things too terrible to mention

i do not want to talk myself out of this or any other
calamity   i warn the sand crabs about
such linguistic solutions the way my father
warned me but he was oceanographic and I know
that sailors are not easily lured
by tongue   scratchy barnacle
that remote

the source of our malice for sea life is clear
if you remember the turbulence of amniotic fluid

even the otter has questionable ethics
you can't trust anything that eats on its back

either in or out of water   it is hard
to imagine humans surviving much of anything

go ahead, submerge your hands in the black water of the spillway
to feel any affection for that which no longer reaches the sea

the competition between salt and sky cannot dazzle hawk
or dissuade us from our battles with atmosphere
the nuclear cloud of memory is prehistoric knowledge, is deep water
we surface by burning prairie grass and pygmy rabbit
drawing the smoke up into ourselves
when night falls we are still damp from hatching
the crickets warn of the moon's entanglements
a towering monument overshadowing rock and river
we are woman and ox, our legs a muscular paradise of blue

to cross time is not
to mark its curvature
but its scales
the crepuscular death
of iridescent things opening
in this moment which has happened
has not happened
not exactly brilliant but lingering
we make months of ourselves
weeks take days   call it luck or sarsaparilla
the past has no referent but scent
sweet is not unlike bitter when you bite down on it
a hummingbird is such a femme thing
but she can hurt you too

this morning is not the witch's tit that you spoke of. so many disastrous women or so the story goes. there are others who claim not to notice the circumstance of sex. i call them liars but i know enough never to do this to their face. the earth as mother is a tragedy of subjugation and resistance. twenty miles away dawn is met by a concrete freeway overpass where she wakes, her body some broken antique toy. some parts move noisily. the others time has frozen in place. go ask her what woman means, mother or pleasure or garbage strewn contiguously so that no one place is either landfill or pristine. not containment or contaminant but that which bears the brunt of it, some dark once-furry place between her legs.

in the beginning people said all kinds of things
which later someone took for religion
but the first words were not about god but food
then sex i know because i've been hungry
god has nothing to do with it
when the ocean comes and reclaims us
a few will survive, they will eat and make babies
this is my story and god is not allowed
only tangerines and sailor girls
there will be no more babies either

the sea is such longing for
its young, dawn, that pocked beauty
we have switched our alliance
made family out of desert
desiccant, this relative of
thirsty enough to swallow
our rage, her mouth, spitting out
cactus and scree, impervious to the hunger
wrinkled sheaths of skin

one way to explain it is the tree
those skinny roots stabbing into volcanic rock
the first thing to grow isn't always pretty
the limbs are barren sticks
there are no flowers or fragrant music
it is simply phloem and xylem
emerging from the crust
an igneous womb

WORST CASE:
WATER

No one will be there to remind you to breathe. Do not panic when your body breaks through the ice to the shock of water below. There may be birds or a marmot skating past. Do not be confused by the blurring of horizon and sky. Focus all of your intention on the ice. In it is the message, the moral. If the ice is cloudy and scattered, you may not survive. This is a lesson in paying attention. If the ice is its own continent, if you taste it and it is salty and dry, then you might. Either way it is best to kick your legs and heave yourself toward the sky. If you cannot lift yourself out of the freezing water, you should call on the spirit world. There are supernatural possibilities. Ask Sky to help you. She is the end and the beginning. If you do not know her true name, you may call her whatever you like. The world has been renamed before. It has caused humans a great deal of suffering. But Sky understands. Humans depend on language. Sky depends on nothing at all.

NOMENCLATURE,
MIIGAADIWIN,
A FORKED TONGUE

ADZE:

I should begin with adik, with herding mammals ranging across
the boreal expanse. To know the geography of it, to start with
its features.

Your face is this blur of fur and antler.

My story is the history of frontier, a wooded terrain. We could not
see each other through the cacophony of trees. But I could hear you
breathing. Some kind of wind the nose sings. Adze is stripping the
layers of. When the skin is torn from muscle, cleaved from bone.

Agawaatese is not sound but shadow. An interception of light.

BAGIJIGAN:

Offering. I have only this. A life without footprints.

From the rooftop anything is possible. Free of ground and its gravities, there is no track of your departure. I found a book of two tongues from which I describe twilight. I too am this in-between thing.

Miziwekamig is not earth. It is adverb; it is strewn about and across. Aki is the name by which the earth is called in secret, what I would have whispered into the soft yield of your belly if you had remained. Now, alone, I could call the world akiiwan, this celestial body. To be gravity and mass, to cling to what you know. I would have given you this, my slippery tongue, but you were walking backward toward the edge of the rooftop. Beyond you was the emptiness of horizon, asphalt, another inanimate future self.

CAPITAL:

Dawn is not self referential. Neither is dusk. If I could speak this,
if I could, anishinaabe-gaagiigido.

I know only what language makes possible. A tenuous transmission
of. I could describe it as inendaagozi or inendaagwad, but meaning
is something else entirely. To be remembered is not to hold the
idea of oneself, some bundled thing wrapped against the cold.

You once said that nouns were for accumulation, for bartering and
trade. Use everything you can, you said. I have laid out all my assets
on the rooftop. There is some duplication, an echoing of. In which
language should I describe the different parts of me? Inzid, nininj,
there is another.

By dusk the buzzards blanket the sky overhead. But my body is less
remarkable absent of blood.

I have sorted the dismembered pieces of me according to their
function. Appendage is crowded, but indengway has no one beside
her. What can one do with a face? Peel back the skin and her
features are indistinguishable. Remove nishkiinzhigoon and, now
sightless, she is without point of view.

DISTAFF:

In old English there is always some German lingering about.
I've named the residual Hans and given him a theatrical side.
Anishinaabemowin is Maude at the turn of the century. My little
bear girl. She is small and dark with a deep guttural laugh. Hans is
no match for her.

I begin each day at the spinning wheel. You would call this women's
work. But it is Hans whose fingers thread the yarn. Before the end
eclipsed the beginning, there was an infinite thread. No one could
say where it began and where it ended. No one tied themselves up
in little knots.

When Maude wakes she finds Hans with blood-stained fingers. She
washes the stains from his niibinaakwaanininjiin, those fragile cups.

Is the story the same without the thread of history? I would ask
you, but your past has erased your present. Someone once said that
aesthetics are for those without adult responsibilities. Or was it
ethics? I always had trouble telling them apart.

EDAWAYI'II:

There are many ways to tell both sides of it. It is a preposition.

The French mated their way through the colonies. The English claimed only their mirror image. Later the science of alterity would explain such predilections. Absent of Freud, native kinship systems did not distinguish between the progeny of.

Halfbreeds have their own word for gichi-mookomaan, for white person, for butcher knife. Little bear girl took the knife and split herself down the middle. Little bear girl sits beside me on the rooftop, her hair scissoring the wind. Together we watch flora and fauna duck for cover. One is the hydrology of earthquakes, the other less tectonic, more personal. Gichi-mookomaan is nowhere to be found.

It is difficult to be part of a species. There is so little to distinguish yourself from. Sapiens traveled slowly across continents, moved from trees to terra firma. At which point did gichi-mookomaan roam?

They have paved the surface of our habitat, but someday they too will long for the upper canopy. Bipedalism is a fetish of the imperial view.

FEAST:

In every story of catastrophe, there is a wiikonge which brings the
people together. You would call it the ritual of disarmament. But
when we met, you hungered for my spleen. The pilgrims hungered
for everything. They almost starved.

After the feast, there is always regret. The pilgrims regretted
everything they did not steal.

In the spring, when the earth was just beginning itself anew, they
renamed it waabooz and stripped it of its skin. You stripped me
of everything else. Later, you would regret leaving me for I was
banajaanh and still nestling.

I've learned that we are all small, insignificant things.

> To the wind, there is this fragile expanse of
> wing. To each other, we are what we do not say
> aloud, maanadikoshens, horned and reckless.

To be the same is bezhigwan, an inanimate, intransitive thing.
I call the world something other than place; I call it bimikawaan.
To err is to misread symptom as source. Errors are rampant.

GRAMMAR:

No language considers itself part of another. It is not just the
eyes or lips or the fault line cleaving muscle from earth, its bone.
We are gookoosh and zhiishiib, mammal and bird, between us a
separate evolution.

> The word for love is similar to the word for
> spill, for sweeping past the bank. To be married is
> wiidige, to live together, held by the bows of birch.
> To be legally married is something different; it
> requires a license, an Indian official, things that
> came later, food rations, theft, disease.

In winter, the warmth of your bed was wiidige, to be hooked
around the body of another. The snow was blind to semantic
distinctions. The sensation of flushed skin was the same, woman
or man, ninaabem or wife. Call it doodooshaaboo and drink.

HYSTERIA:

I've been called worse. In a time overly attentive to the interiority
of artificial spaces, any reference to the womb seems sentimental.
Mine is barren, a forgotten thing. I've named her gwiingwa'aage;
she is almost extinct.

Despite the loss of species, the science of biology has forged ahead.
The modern biomedical model can now predict our future cell
by cell. I've begun a collection of fingernail clippings, deciduous
hairs, an arsenal of DNA. This has not lessened the instances
of giiwanaadizi, of hunger, of madness, but it has created the
possibility of a predictable future self. People used to have similar
worries about psychology, all those methods for reading the
language of one another's pathos. But pathology is now restricted
to the laboratory of the body. It's a good thing that Freud is dead.
He would seem so archaic, all that talk of obsession and desire.

The wolverine too was called gluttonous. Now she waits.
Gwiingwa'aage curled tight in the arc of the womb.

IDIOM:

To be distinctive. To mean more than the words themselves can
convey. He was this and other than. He was awakaan.

She was the artifice of manners, a china cabinet, hunting from her blind.

He told stories with himself cast as the protagonist in the lives of
other people. He was old then, certain we children would never
know the difference. While he slept, she made certain corrections.
Yes gizhaadigewinini, we said, for she was our keeper. She told us the
stories belonged to some and not others. She decided when and which
animal would be killed.

Being part of her semantic family restricted his meaning to only what
was shared. Truth is a muddling of. I was ten and could not fathom
the woods, the frozen bodies, the monstrous wiindigoo who ate the
meat of humans and left their blood smeared bones in the snow.
These are the tales a grandfather tells to his abinoojiinyag. But the
wiindigoo is not a mythical figure. Terrible, human and not, he is the
flesh eater who lies in wait inside us all.

Starvation is not the only act of malevolence. There is also maji-
manidoo, the violence of family relations. She inhabited his
dreams, stole his past, changed his story. In the end, she made him
colloquial. But he had the power to foretell his grandchildren's future.
Wiisaaakodewininiwag, he said of all his progeny for he too had been
split and bound by centuries of copulation and war.

JAAGA'E:

It is true, I have spent all my ammunition. I am unarmed on the
rooftop, the site of your absence from.

Below the world is its own clamoring. When akiwenzii settles in
the doorway, he fills it with his accumulation, a lifetime of. I am
not the only one watching. Behind the flowered curtain is my
neighbor, a woman whose life is a fearful surveillance. A half an
hour later, the police have come.

I am like mizise, an awkward bird hovering.

The world repeats itself. A policeman kicks akiwenzii's legs, which
in sleep have protruded beyond the shadow of the doorway. I shout
from the rooftop, Nimishoo, but akiwenzii does not hear me.
Another man takes out his nightstick and waves it across the spread
of disastrous belongings. Akiwenzii gathers his legs, but does not
flinch. Every uniform is a reference to its violent origin. Akiwenzii
is old enough to know the etymology.

Nimishoo is the one whose own family called him other. His
mother said as much, even without the stink of history on her
breath. When he was twelve, his uncle gave him a pet lizard and
a waagikomaan, something to split the life from. For his gifts,
uncle made certain requests. Simple things really—a touch, a brief
opening. Only later did Nimishoo learn to read his life according
to the shape of another man's intestines.

Who can say what it means to be spent, emptied of.

In one move, akiwenzii lifts himself to his knees and draws the knife across the man's waist. He holds the mess of entrails as a talisman against the other. Nimishoo knows the world is flat. More than once, he has fallen off.

KINDERGARTEN:

So many mornings of misplaced identity, hours searching beneath
the bed.

The first day of school caused a collision of selves; there were too
many to fit inside the narrow sleeves of my new uniform.

The days were spent amidst wall-to-wall carpet and storybooks.
Strange adults spoke to us in a language that was neither ours nor
theirs, a no-one's tongue.

Young enough to be curious and curious enough to be bad, I led
the other children during recess into the darkness of the closet.
Crouching beneath the enormous coats that adults cloaked
themselves in, I would put my fingers in every orifice. I was taller
then and always bossy. My teacher called me disobedient, but I called
myself zhaangweshi, and taught the boys and girls to pet my silky fur.

Later there were fewer selves and less pleasure in.

At home on the rooftop, I have constructed a closet to call my own.
Inside, I recite unintelligible nursery rhymes, tales of beanstalks
and old women living in shoes. I stroke myself, my zhaangweshi,
and remember the pleasure of those small bodies, supple and
quivering beside my own.

LAMENT:

To be gathered together under one roof, to be staked and hobbled. We are stabled by the limits of.

To be american is to be gichi-mookomaan, a country of. Such isolate objects. For five hundred years, there were generations whose sole purpose was to split and swallow. They broke the continent into states, into fragments of.

> We people, the first people. Our word for ourselves is the word for our tongue. There is no difference between the naming and those being named; language calls the world into being. But americans have been burdened with the difficult translation from self to other. It made them dangerous.

We people have become ozhaawashko, adjectival, a bruised face, an injured mare. It is the only word to approximate this moment, here in the stall, with little room to move in any direction. But my ancestors remember and in this way we work ourselves backward. We were not born bebezhigooganzhii, hoofed and swoop-backed. Of whatever state, we were once free.

MOHAWK:

Before the Sex Pistols there were other markers of resistance.
Take the state of Connecticut for instance, all those nice puritans
and their heretical belief in a dour god. Who can blame them for
their fear of extravagantly shaved heads, of beautifully decorated
objects of the mundane. Of axes. After the skirmishes, there
would be bedroom communities. Long cocktail hours. What
woods remained were like the houses, crops of uniform height and
dimension. Teenagers began shaving their heads in defiance of
the repetition. Few saw the irony. They were the inheritors of this
great promise: freedom to worship a life unfettered by sacrament.
But miigaadiwin is ritual and death. Beneath the elegant suburban
houses, the earth is fallow with human bones.

NISHKOONZH:

My snout is jeweled and feral. An inheritance of sorts. After the earth was split in two, there were stitches running its length. This is a story of trains, of buffalo and saloons. Nishkoonzh is this scent of things.

> To know is to be reminded of. A smell that lingers. I am here and I am a hundred years earlier. I will tell you a secret. My snout knew which trains to chase, which passengers had hunted from their pillowed seats at the window. When the train stopped, I split them open with my claw, as the earth had been split, buffalo blood seeping into its wounds.

The earth was once wrapped and porous, a kind of skin. We are nishiime, what came later. When all of the children were taken, the skin puckered and dried. This is why the last buffalo hides in the mountainside. The earth is scarred, a saloon scabbing at every injury. Now is the time of nishiwe, of killing what remains.

OPTICS:

The science of sight ignores the spirit of mescaline, of cactus, of natives of the new world.

> After the earth split, there were two, old and new. The old world was heavy with everything that began it. The new world was fecund, virile.

When the first people came out of the trees they found themselves on a wooded island already crowded with bear and wolf. Stripping bark from the trees, they built canoes and paddled to the other side.

When light moves through solid particles it loses pieces of itself. It is altered once it reaches its destination.

Omoodayaabik is shattered, a piece of broken glass. Before it could have been anything: a lantern, a window, a bottle of whiskey. The science of sight does not trouble itself with such inquiries. There are only the intricacies of the eye, its mechanics of doing. The eye does not know which side of the earth it is on. The eye cannot see the birthing folds, the suckled nipples beneath the limbs of trees. The nose is far less complicated. There is no discipline dedicated solely to its mysteries. But it is the nose that remembers our disastrous origins. We are sentient. We are this scent of things.

POSSESS:

We have tried to codify each calamity in order to present time in
equal measure from beginning to end. I have grown tired of this
chronology. Reckless, I turn to the depth gauge and the shovel.
Archeology requires the absence of unrecorded interventions, a
world without mamigaade or theft. With one robust thrust, I have
rearranged history, burying plastic robotics beneath centuries
of the ubiquitous earthenware. In the presence of such science
fiction, what story can the future make?

QUELL:

One quarter of rams prefer the horned, the horny male of their
species. Older studies of human mammalian behavior found
something closer to one in ten. What the ewe desires is anybody's
guess. If you shear her coat of wool you will find tender pink flesh.
Beneath your coat, you are desiccant, unyielding. You are that
which cannot, won't. To quell is to rattle until the pen breaks.
The ewe will choose her own direction. She is warm and fat. Her
whiteness is bright against the green hills. Maanishtaanish has
been called simple, docile, flock. But she is alone and grazing
toward the mountain's spine. When night calls the wolves howl.
She tucks her legs beneath her white coat and dreams of men,
penned and naked, bleating like sheep.

RECUSANT:

England has inspired many rebellions. Something about the
dampness, the fog and stone. When the colonies threw off their
master, the penchant for boiled potatoes remained. I do not
worship in the Church of England, but I was baptized by the hands
of its descendants. I can still name all of jesus' disciples, describe
every betrayal.

If I were a comic this would be a funny story. If I were catholic
the baptism would have been followed by an enormous feast.
Protestants distrust pleasure. Ojibweg distrust protestants. This is
celebrated annually. On thanksgiving, whoever has the most boiled
potatoes wins. Salvation is measured by the number of potatoes in
each pot.

Jiibaakwewakik is the cooking pot. If you empty the pot and turn it
on its rim, the black marks will tell your future. Too much soot and
only the jiibay can say.

Gichi-mookomaanag built houses on top of human graves. Their
pots tell them nothing. They can't hear a single word that anyone
else has to say.

SCYTHE : GIISHKIZHIGAN

There have been many massacres. They pock the earth, a constellation to guide you. When you were seven, you tied a boy to a tree and left him there. There was no malice in this experiment. The boy was home by supper. Later you lit a car on fire. Other than the charred front seats, there were no injuries. Cause and effect were difficult lessons for you to learn.

Once grown, you became bimaaji'aad, more heroic. Sometimes a scythe is a weapon, sometimes giishkizhigan is a tool. Captain Cook was sacrificed to the gods he scorned, his bloody heart offered up as an apology. General Custer died of malnutrition and gunshot wounds. His heart remained untouched.

When Kah-ge-ga-gah-bowh died, he was destitute and alone, but his heart was crowded with christianity. An Ojibwe, Kah-ge-ga-gah-bowh, wrote the story of his conversion from savage to salvation, from Kah-ge-ga-gah-bowh to George Copway. A few years after the emancipation proclamation, the Indian converted from protestantism to catholicism. Catholics have an infinite number of saints. Copway had only the story of himself to guide him. The red child of the forest believed evil spirits could make him sick. Later, a christian, he believed only the devil had the power to do such things.

TOTEM:

On the rooftop I have sculpted your life as symbol. Excised the
image of. Because you left me. Because I can.

You called yourself wooden, scarred. Now you are carved stone.
I wrap your midsection with twine and place on it an offering. In
this way you become an altar, a special place on the mantle of my
lean-to.

Bound in the ritual of my disbelief, you are merely a figure of. And
like all figures, you are hungry for a meaning beyond your own.

UVULA:

Little grape is not herself today. She has discovered the irritant will never be a pearl. Uva would cry but she is too old for such things.

When my tongue split, the earth was broken in two. Zhawimin is uva on the backside of the world.

Zhawimin writes herself each day anew. When the dawn breaks Zhawimin is light. By dusk she is liquid, a maple weeping.

I put my tongue to the bark, lick the damp flesh. Little grape is the breath beside me. Zhawimin calls her sister vain and territorial. Uva dismisses such criticisms as dishonorable.

If I could tie myself back together they would not call each other rival. Once the mirrors are all covered, we will be able to return to the caves of the underworld.

The mouth is one such place. Little grape was born in the center of it. She hangs there night after night, remembering the first prayer. Zhawenjige, she whispers, and there in the hiss of her breath is the possibility of mercy.

VARMINT:

I first learned the history of nomenclature when I was still
mistaking myself for a boy. All of the names I gave to myself, to the
various parts of me, turned out to be wrong. So much seemed to
hinge on the swell of my breasts. I named one adik and the other
adze. They hunted one another. Later there was a war. Miigaadiwin
is not ashamed of the damage he caused. Miigaadiwin is the boy
in the heart of the girl. When Crazy Horse was killed, the soldiers
took him to a jail cell and stripped him naked. Beneath his robe,
they discovered the genitals of a girl. Gichi-mookomaanag have
always been afraid of contradictions. When I was born, my parents
discovered a large clitoris and tiny vaginal folds. I do not blame
them for their confusion. It had been over a hundred years since
my people had lived anishinaabe-bimaadizi. It had been longer
than anyone could recall. As a child, I learned the names for
things that were made from the death of what came before. New
words had to be created to describe everything gichi-mookomaanag
destroyed. I have taken to calling every battle varmint. But
miigaadiwin prefers zhagashkaandawe, disguising his violence
in its winged fur.

WIIKWAJI'O:

I am not trying anything at all.

Actions are measured by the arc of their displacement. I have
displaced myself in order to follow your shadow. But you are hazy
and witching, coated beneath the liquidity of my own dissolution.
To say this is to further the misrepresentation. No translation can
echo wiikwam, sucking my life through this fissure, a forked tongue.

There is an art to this, to all things partial and approximate.

Wiikwajitoon is shame and grief, what I am trying to unburden
myself of. Not every subject requires an object but all stories
require a listener. I have trapped you here as memory. I have tied
you to the mantle of.

Once we were cross-cousins, a flirting kinship. Our marriage was
forbidden. Wiikwaji'o is trying to rid myself of desire.

Gichi-mookomaan calls the longing illness, prescribes abstinence,
another lifetime barefoot on the balcony. But you are aniibiishaa-
bookewinini and beyond the bounds of such prescriptions. Your
feet were cobbled in your youth.

XYLEM:

The layers of. When I was born I was a hollow quill, a miigwan free of wing and tail, an empty vessel to call my own.

> Tell me anishinaabeg
> about the wind
> that brings you
> hovering, this
> wooded ancestry.

When I was born my parents stripped a hawk of its feathers. It never flew again. Xylem was once the food and fluid of. I was once slippery with your juice. But I've had my fill of you; I've hardened and dried, my limbs desiccant, wanagek. The quill cannot write itself free of its hollowness. The story will always be concave, a collapse against which another tale forms.

Miigwan is the girl about whom nothing should be told. She is neither sacred nor taboo. She is merely a child who will grow up to be another gatherer, these unwoven strings.

YA'AW : YO'O

In between
nesting.

The owl is not
my enemy.

Its call does not
signal the end of
anything other
than,

You are winter
this flight of.

Beneath your shadow
is another.

Blood, a splattering
the ubiquitous snow.

ZIIGINIGEWIGAMIG:

Autopsy is a western fixation, a belated curiosity about the body of.

When her body is split and dismembered, she cannot be found inside. To be spirit and flesh. To leave the flesh behind.

When the bartender asked her if she had enough money to pay for the drink she had ordered, she said "if the spirits want me they can have me for free."

If you looked up you would notice what hovers above, beyond our reach. The sky is not empty. There are hooks and ropes. She has long since been dangling from.

At the edge of the reservation, every reservation, is the ziiginigewigamig. She was fourteen when she first sat at the bar and ordered a whiskey. No one asked her to pay a dime. The men had wasted their lives waiting for her. Above her barstool was a meat hook, slack and bloody. She saw it in the reflection of the akiwenziiyag, in yoke of their eyes. It took many years for her to reach it. By then all the akiwenziiyag were strung up high.

The autopsy tells us only what has failed in her, which organs have bloated to twice their normal size. There is another story, another picture of.

When the earth is mined of all its treasures, the land will be barren. But the sky will be crowded with bodies. When the limp appendages slap against one another, there is a second sound, less percussive. It is her, raptor, this cry.

WORST CASE:
EARTH

Between dawn and dusk each tree is distinct. The bark, the leaves, the spider webs spun between the branches. If you close your eyes you can hear them humming. The oak makes a sound several octaves lower than the pine. Alders are sopranos. Once it is dark their voices blend. The trunks all look the same. The bats move in a way that confuses you. They hear their way through the darkness. You rely on sight. Follow the howl of the coyotes. They prefer open vistas. If you are lucky, they will call forth the moon and in her white light, you will feel safe. The next day will be easier. You will know that the night alone cannot kill you. Remember this when you find the way back to your car, your job, your life. The city is not absent of music. Open your apartment window. Listen to the children playing in the school yard, the shouting of the couple across the way, the ambulance screaming past. When you close your eyes, you can still see the bank of trees, the dusk of leaves overhead. Sing to them a healing song. They too are animate and far from home.

Do not make any sudden movements. Remember that kid from geometry class who lumbered slowly to his chair. He is on television, the world's slowest mechanic. You should have paid more attention to him. He fixes things until they are perfect, even things that are not broken. He could have fixed you if you had let him. Now you are at the edge of a cliff. The car ran out of gas miles back. You kicked the tires half-heartedly; it wasn't really the car's fault. You knew the gas gauge didn't work. You knew the woman didn't love you. Leave me alone, she said. I am alone, you said. There were problems with communication. The cliff is equally vague about its intentions. It is both terminal and impermanent. From a distance its edges are clearly marked, but when you grab hold of it the earth breaks apart in your hands. Like love, you think. But you mean lust. You have always confused the two. Maria said as much. She wouldn't even open the door for you. You had to stand in the courtyard while she lectured you from her apartment window. She was beautiful in the lamplight, but her mouth was moving. You waved goodbye to her, to disappointment. It wasn't long before the car ran out of gas. You walked for almost an hour in the darkness before reaching the cliff. Once you found the edge, you forgot why you had come. You are always forgetting things, like why Maria refuses to love you. If you had any gas you would drive back and ask her. Instead, you sit in the darkness near the edge of the cliff moving your hands through the crumbling earth. If you had paid more attention in geometry you would know the formula for this. You could predict when the edge would be directly beneath you. That boy would know. But then he would not have run out of gas. He would not have loved a woman like Maria. He would have fixed the whole mess a long time ago.

There are seven bison remaining in California. They live on the slope of an excavated hill. At dawn they cluster together on the western edge of fence. There is no mountainside for them to hide in. White Buffalo Calf Woman gave the Lakota the sacred pipe. She was wakan and could not be harmed by arrow or bullet. The people had other weapons. She gave them seven sacred rituals and then disappeared into the white cloud of their disbelief. There are seven bison and 36,457,549 people in California. The largest terrestrial mammal in North America, the bison live in a paddock the size of a city block. Darkly furred and humped, bison can survive for up to 20 years. In captivity their lives are more precarious; they suffer from alcoholism, poverty, a sickness of spirit. 60 million bison once roamed the grasslands of North America. There are seven circling their pen. There is only one way to tell you this. We are endangered. Current rates of depensation make it unlikely that we will ever recover.

A NEW ORDER OF

DOMAIN

Lanky and feathered, buzzard attempted to gather firelight. Some animals said bear had it. Others said fire was a dream that hadn't been dreamed yet.

To call it yours. To call anything proprietary. What it means to be sentient, to be afraid.

Spider thought her web into being. She had the light of the moon, but she too craved fire. Elaborate in her arrangement of limbs, she set off toward the amber horizon. The other animals nodded at her bravery, their eyes following her into the periphery.

All biological systems are porous, dependent, upon some kind of exchange. When spider brought back fire, her once black back pulsed with a new orange light.

Physics has its own explanation for things. For them, there is neither buzzard nor spider, but always there is fire. Without it there would be no alchemy, no chemistry, no way to alter the elemental states of being.

Imagine the world is in fact cleaved, a split in spider's back. Beneath the red glow is a viscous fluid. Swim into to it. It is amniotic. Breathe through the porous cells of your skin.

KINGDOM

There are four families of primates in the new world. Scientists believe that platyrrhini migrated across the Atlantic Ocean to South America some 40 million years ago on a raft of mangrove. New world monkeys differ from old world monkeys primarily in the nose and teeth. Platyrrhini is flat nosed with twelve premolars instead of eight. These were formed after months of eating only the bark of the mangrove raft. Even now platyrrhini sometimes hangs from the limbs of trees by her teeth. But it is the prehensile tail, that most wondrous limb, that makes the new world primate so strange to behold. Up there in the tree she is beckoning you with a flick of her tail. It is as strong as your arm but more supple, the surface soft with fur. If you could, you would swing yourself up to her. You are the same order but a different family. You lack the arboreal. She is preternaturally flirtatious. This should serve as a warning to you. But you are entranced by the movement of her furred appendage. Come, she says, and somehow without limb or flight you do.

PHYLUM

The Americas span eight percent of the earth's surface. Everywhere, there is water. You are all wetness, some tearing of. This is only a phenomenon of the body. Your mind has utterly left you alone. What it is to be sentient and not sapient. To hold oneself subjectively but lack apperception, that tingling sensation at the base of your neck. In desperation, South America broke free of the supercontinent Gondwanaland. Then came the volcanoes, the endless erosion. An entire world was formed. When you let her inside of you, you became isthmus, this fingering of. Later she would dredge you, make a canal of your intestines, sail clear through.

Amerigo Vespucci renamed himself after Amerike, a merchant who financed explorations across the oceanic expanse. To be closer to the continents. To be of and from. To be with her and to forget everything else. To hold her and name this geography as your own.

The Americas are rimmed with mountains. Between lay vast plains. In the north, there are protestants everywhere. Even the immense river basin cannot wash the land free of them. What has been sacrificed still bleeds in the mountainside. The rest is leeched white. A blanketing or blizzard of. This hungering of the new world.

CLASS

There are many means of differentiation. To order yourself according to. To sort, then judge. Taxonomy is a hierarchical arrangement. You learned this early, but somehow misunderstood hierarchy's relationship to gender. Who could imagine that the parameters of girlhood could be so narrow? This is a problem of being. Some make a study of it; others fuck their way through. The knowledge of how is always more fun than the knowledge of why. In either case the nomenclature differs, but the effect is the same.

Pay attention to the color and texture of your tongue. This is predictive; it is diagnostic. In the center strip is a narrow groove. Many have been caught in it. Sometimes your mouth is too full to chew. This is how you learn the limits of your heart. When she follows the curve of you there is both slippage and some wooded place, what birds hatch the sky into. You call yourself wing, a feathering, but cannot navigate the wind. Any impediment really is enough to make you forget your own classification.

Without order there is some confusion about cause and effect. But you will always have metaphor. Somewhere in this juxtaposition is the capacity to transform. Your tongue riot with. Each exhalation, the birth of another century, its violent form.

WORST CASE:
METAL AND FIRE

How many times did your mother tell you to cover yourself, your nose, your ears, to protect yourself from cold? Close your mouth, she said. Shut your damn orifices. When the temperature drops below fifty degrees your asshole contracts. This alone will not protect you. Your skin, that enormous organ, is porous. The cold moves through your body like night, born by wind and rain. When your body temperature drops cold blood pools in your extremities. Eventually you become tired and disoriented. Your mother, that bitch, tell her you were wearing a fucking hat. Do not rub your numb extremities. Do not slip into unconsciousness. Where is your mother? Ask her to draw you a scalding bath. Dangle your extremities over the lip of the bathtub. You do not want the cold blood to rush back toward your heart. Keep your anger close. Ask her where the hell she was when you needed her. She is busy scrubbing the dirt from behind your ears. Your genitals are burning and your toes are numb. You see the child in the bathtub, scrubbed clean by her mother's hands. You see the rain turn to hail. You are miles from anything, anyone. You should build a shelter. Light a fire. Instead you lay down on the wet earth beneath a tree. You should sleep. Yes, the only thing to do is sleep.

The room will be larger or smaller than you expected. Do not act surprised. Everything you think should remain a secret. Screaming will not help you. You are here for a reason. Even the minor offenses add up. Remember the day you clipped the elderly man with your cart in the supermarket aisle? He stumbled, almost fell. He looked so much like that asshole uncle of yours that you couldn't stop yourself. Then there are all those recyclable bottles you just threw away. They are buried somewhere, some enormous landfill. Or maybe they are on a barge, mounds of garbage floating out to sea. The metal is both smooth and rough against your arms. It was probably the woman in the alley you walked by so many mornings. She was always sick. You began to walk the long way to work just to avoid the sound of her retching. Why shouldn't there be some kind of reckoning? The pipe is without judgment. There were acts of generosity. The day you picked up two hitchhikers, a man and his son, and gave them each an orange. The woman in the alley was beyond your help. You were always taught to avoid no-win situations. There is no solution to the garbage. The old man was fine, a little bruised maybe. Concentrate on the rope. It is porous. Sweat as much as you can.

INHERITANCE

LEGACY

The woman at the Native American Cultural Center wears her Indian
proudly. The earrings are turquoise but she is Creek, a member of
the Cherokee Nation. You are harder to recognize. One grandfather
who headed west two years before the state of dispossessed Chippewa
formed their own federally recognized tribe. He left everything of
his heritage behind. You came later, at a time without tribe, family,
your Native tongue. You withstand the genealogy exercise, smile,
tell what you know, apologize for what you do not. She is kind, she
will embrace you, but she wants to know what kind of Indian you are
first. This is both old and new. Lineage is important; blood lines
define clans, delineate tribal communities. But blood quantum
is new. Established by the government in 1934, it is one of many
gifts of the Indian Reorganization Act whose purpose is to define
membership, restrict recognition, effect the eventual termination of
federally recognized tribes. It is how you end up being a fraction of.
The rules not withstanding, the Creek woman introduces you to the
others as if you are one of them. But when you leave the Center, by
virtue of blood law, you are already disappeared.

THE WATCHING

It was her job, she knew to watch the boy, her brother, her twin. And she did. But the afternoon came when she forgot. They were at the beach. It was not especially pretty, but it was close to the city and the ocean breeze brought some relief from the August heat. They had learned to swim young, but like all things, she was better at it than he. Watch your brother, the mother said, then went to the concession stand for a drink. The mother returned a half hour later while the lifeguard was pulling him out of the water. Driving back into the city, the son curled into a ball like a small animal. The daughter cried, said she was sorry. The mother said nothing.

Later the mother stopped drinking, but the son inherited both the desire and the disease. When he drank himself nearest to death, the daughter flew across the country to be with him. The other chair in the hospital room was empty; the mother could not be reached. That day at the beach, he said, I was only trying to catch up with you. She could feel him dying and a part of her dying too. It was me, she said, I forgot that we are one and the same.

KARMA

Everyone has at least two, she said. She said a lot of things. I believed some of them, none of them. The last time she was just as beautiful, but more naïve. Like you, she said, meaning whomever she was speaking to. When he left her for the blue expanse of ocean, she had thrown herself over the balustrade. Can you believe it, she said, I shattered and he simply sailed away. She told me she had learned her lesson. She swore off men, romance, any elevated surface. That's where I came in. Petite, I was catlike, ermine. She called me ocelot, then kissed me. Her lips were soft but my tongue got caught on her rail of broken teeth.

RESENTMENT

To let go of it, she offered her palms to the sky, as if sky wanted such things: resentment, grief, the myriad of human attachments. Later the sky made its own offering, freezing rain that fell in perfectly round pellets of ice. She put a glass bowl down outside her front door to gather it. In the morning, she found a black dog peeing into the frozen bowl.

PASSING

When she was born she developed a cough that wouldn't go away, some kind of damp lung thing that made her vulnerable to others. Or at least that is the story her parents told to explain why she never left the house until she was far too old to learn how to live among others. When she asked about the physical differences—the soft fur on her ears, the way her chin drew out rather than down—they waved their hands as if her concerns were flies bothering the air.

Now she is older and her parents are dead but she is still home, sitting in the window, looking out longingly at the open field and the road that winds like a river beyond. One day she packs a bag and leaves, walking the curves of the asphalt bank until she reaches town. Entering the first open door she finds, she is surprised by the room of welcoming faces that greet her. Either she is passing as something they might learn to love, or she has been one of them all along.

THE OLDEST ONE AT THE PIG ROAST

It is hard to know for sure the age of anyone in the dark. The pig, fully grown and fattened with hormones, could not be more than 10 months old. The others, the ones drinking around the fire pit, are probably closer to twenty-five. This would make her the chaperone, but she is drinking too, heavily like they are, drinking vodka and whatever mixture of juice was on the table next to it. She can smell the pig cooking, the scent of it roasting in its own juices, and she knows that she will not be able to remain quietly among them. It is not just age, or the generations of wealth they wear as if a second skin. It is that she finally understands that without her, without the exception of her presence, the series of accessible achievements that mark their lives would seem privileged. But she is here, a member of the not-disappeared, a people only partially counted in the census until 1930. And so, their success can be narrated differently. It is a meritocracy after all. The rest is just history. She drinks two more drinks, says a blessing for the slaughtered pig, and begins the dance that centuries ago someone mistook for a welcome. It is not. It is what her people danced when it is was time for the gichi-mookomaanags to sail back home.

BROKER

Friday afternoon, late in the recession, there is a line at the pawnshop. The woman at the counter is selling her childhood earrings, the wedding coins sprinkled, so many years ago, over her and her new husband's bowed heads. He is dead now, as is the child she used to be. The broker gives her one hundred and seventy-five dollars. She thanks him although it won't get her through the week. Next, the broker calls, and the man in line empties the entire content of his pockets on the glass. The quarters scatter as if a tumble of jewels. American quarters, copper and nickel, and he has twenty of them. The broker smiles, kind considering the line. These are quarters sir, he says. The man nods; he is at a coin shop. OK, the broker says, for this one, the 1985 issue, I'll give you twenty-five cents.

At the bottom of your purse is a one ounce gold coin your grandmother gave you. It is not an heirloom. It is a South African Kruger Rand from 1979, a year alight with bombs that, despite the laws, could not distinguish race and often killed whites and blacks alike. The Kruger Rand sells for thirteen hundred dollars. Seven times what it was purchased for. It is an easy exchange, a brilliant gold coin, heavy with oppression and the violence of extraction, and a check, thin paper striped blue and gray through which money is made formal, benign. You are not catholic, not even religious, but walking out of the shop you make the sign of the cross, ask god to forgive you. Two doors down, there is a bar crowded with happy-hour revelers. With so many unemployed, the end of the work week merits a celebration of both its existence and its culmination.

On the sidewalk out front are four or five people smoking next to a sign that tells them not to. There is a code to live by, you know, and yet you no longer are able to make out the words.

WORST CASE:
AIR

The elevator is the last frontier. There are Indians and buffalo. Bring your shotgun and something to roast over the fire. You are Custer and Geronimo, Red Bull and General Jackson. You are in an elevator. You may not breed. The buffalo are waiting in the mountainside. The Indians are inside your skin. There are two types of elevators, hydraulic and cable, of which the hydraulic is most likely to fall. You are in an elevator. The lights go out. Someone is breathing beside you. When the elevator door closed, you were alone. Now you are not. We all carry our relatives inside of us. When the elevator falls, drop to your stomach; cover your head. Don't worry about the person breathing beside you. No one survives an elevator fall. If you die without breeding there will be one less Indian. Indians are important. Without us, team mascots would only be reptiles and four legged mammals. Without us, there would be no popcorn. There was a movie about an Indian. She was guiding the canoe. She was from a different tribe; you wouldn't have understood one another. But she knew better than to get into a hydraulic elevator. That was one of the lessons you lost along the way. The other lesson was more esoteric. Something about humility or was it history. Listen to your ancestor. She is on the floor beside you. She is holding your head in the crook of her arm.

IN SITU

pluvial or pleistocene
fossilized cloak of night
masking population lush as willow
the shadowing, what we
alone   recover

land a narrow tongue nestled
against the sea, rivers swallowing

granite, silt, cyprus roots, her legs
thrust open, a passage among trout, kingfisher

antelope trails snaking the swollen flesh
her mouth opens to hermit thrush, swallow

exhale hawk and bear, the pink salmon
feed only when you are hungry

talk of stubborn children tossed to sky
outline the shape of dusk and wait

they will speak of you always
wretched diggers

seriation

a method of dating
kitchen ware, weaponry, human hair
relative to wind, pollen
drought or slaughter
how they explain so much damage
as if two worlds, empty and full
moving in-between

snow dusts the canyon its seasons of church, people
flushed west as cow replaces buffalo, timid sheep
hunting each other or waiting for the truckloads of men
snow mobiles and shotguns blasting this shape of america, a study
of horse meat and syphilis

wind as white river or charcoal smudged across the page
of trees darkened by ants moving along the nude bark
as small colonies or herds of cattle bend their heads
towards grass buried by snow knowing what lies beneath
but waiting as she waits for him to return or to die
beneath the blanket erasing his shrunken body moving
from one white field to another explosion of snow
the force of desire its nucleus

evidence

A)   Lake Ines and Alba
two sisters who drowned
in the spring the forest
mourned mountain lions
tearing at the cold flesh
raw scar of wood

B)   four point buck shot
with obsidian two inches
from thunder, the coyotes survived
all winter their young nibble the strips
of meat torn like bacon from the deer's
hind legs, clumps of hair
blood, drained free

C)   empty school yard children locked inside tucked behind
desks their toes tapping the wood floor he writes help
with the point of his shoe while the teacher reviews the
vocabulary words he misspelled manipulate but his ears
are their own language of punishment small and
malformed as brussel sprouts the green wounds

archeology

a science of waste and wonder
she weaves baskets of redbud and willow
stitching coils, human intestines

nocharo mu

                          don't touch me

made human by franciscans mapping nudity in wool her newborn
daughter twisting the umbilical cord running her soundless cries
her breast so full of milk she has to stop and bleed her wings
drowning her husband still bent knees in the chapel mouth tacky
with barley soundless prayers his wife in hell the priest tells him
not walking the trail from field to church mourning infant of one
breath even if he feels her next to him at night bound to the bed the
last three months of pregnancy more restless than before only hours
free to birth a world she must bury her fist collapsing landslide

3 wool blankets
3 axes
3 hoes
some clothing
glass beads

antelope   the bowels or entrails
            a severed tongue
        legs

            dangling snow

chronology

another layer of habitation
another back to replace your slip
beneath the weight of

                    fu-sang
                    lip of the pacific
                    silk and brine

sampans rode the black tide
culled abalone   iridescent ears of the sea
could not hear grandmother yee
sing or chong   their erasure
from the record so simple really
to remove the yellow stain

whose name do you carry the sloped shoulders of a father his back
crisp beneath the sun almost purple as a beet his arm still toils
inside of you second cousin to another paper person who harvests
sugar from soil attempt strange frictives with your tongue and
remember he chose this place california is gold mountain this land
its breast and valleys a ghost moaning its limbs breaking apart

an owl cries dusk moon mirrors asphalt as if river a fawn grazes the golf course hungers to test her new found strength she pauses near the stop sign oblivious to its hue must cross between cars maintain an even speed the night a truck turns two wheels airborne one hand in his hair his wife itching the pale scalp the fawn has four legs to contend with two more than she imagines match her stride count them off to yourself her mother taught her rhythm motions her siblings so quick the fawn still straddling the bank and singing night one two bounding across the street one leg bends back she falters three her head turns away from the truck as if only a bird chasing ground her eyes capturing the winged light

soil

burden a rock or the knocking train its roar of moon and stumble
no animal can imitate its reach or bind the miles of tracks
their trust in rows a sick engine runs its own language across mountains
the stitched earth claiming those *wretched heathens*

but not the ones who now traverse land as if history swept clean
as if landscape provided its own erasure or death smoothed the
rough tracks

and echo this diction such an ugly language sound
when darkness is memory and geology
an unnatural burial

NOTES ON NOMENCLATURE

I wrote this series, this alphabet of English and Ojibwe poems, at a time I was recovering so many lost, stolen and forgotten things. I was teaching myself Ojibwe from a dictionary and, in so doing, enacted one of the many ironies of Indigenous peoples' experience: using the cultures and systems responsible for so much of our people's destruction as a link through which I was able to reclaim some of what had been lost.

And yet, this story is not that story, or not only that story. The dictionary that I used, *A Concise Dictionary of Minnesota Ojibwe*, was compiled by John Nichols, a linguistics scholar from the University of Manitoba, and Earl Nyholm, an American Indian Studies professor from Bemidji State University, Minnesota. John Nichols is not Native but he spent decades with the Mille Lacs band of Ojibwe and was eventually adopted by Maude Kess, a prominent tradition bearer of the Ojibwe people. Earl Nyholm is a member of the L'Anse-Baraga band of Ojibwe. The dictionary itself helped birth the Ojibwe People's Dictionary, an online search engine of more than 30,000 words in Central Southwestern Ojibwe, a language now spoken mainly by elders in Minnesota—the land of my grandfather's people—Wisconsin, and Canadian-border lake communities. The Ojibwe People's Dictionary is part of a growing Ojibwe language revitalization effort, which includes immersion schools and classes in many secondary and post-secondary schools throughout Minnesota, Wisconsin, Michigan, and Ontario.

As my grandfather would say, nothing moves in only one direction. That year I spent in my house at the foot of Mount Tamalpais—named by the Coast Miwok people who call this peak their home—reading the dictionary and writing my way toward Ojibwe, I too was part of this larger revitalization project. Although, in the way of so many generations of my family, I did it unknowingly and alone.

I am a writer of apposition and so in Nomenclature the words are placed side by side, Ojibwe and English, English and Ojibwe. And yet their meanings are rarely, if ever, the same. Wittgenstein wrote that "uttering a word is like striking a note on the keyboard of imagination," and for me Ojibwe became a kind of music, a way of hearing the world, its animate and intransitive self.

"Adze"

adik – (na) caribou, reindeer

agawaatese – (vai) cast a shadow flying

"Bagijigan"

bagijigan – (ni) offering

miziwekamig – (pc) all over the world   ~~English~~ Ojibwe

aki – (ni) earth, land, ground, country ~~that which has been taken~~

akiiwan – (vii) to be the earth   she is

"Capital"

anishinaabe-gaagiigido – (vai) to speak in an Indian language; anishinaabe (na) person, human, Indian, Ojibwe

inendaagozi – (vai) to be thought of a certain way, seem to be a certain way, have a certain destiny   ~~living~~

inendaagwad – (vii) to be thought of a certain way, seem to be a certain way   ~~and dead~~

inzid – (nid) my foot

indengway – (nid) my face

nininj – (nid) my hand

nishkiinzhigoon – (nid pl) my eyes

"Distaff"

anishinaabemowin – (ni) Indian language, especially Ojibwe

niibinaakwaanininjiin – (nid) my palm   this body   my own

"Edawayi'ii"

edawayi'ii – (pc) on both sides of it

gichi-mookomaan – (na) white person, american
     inanimate   butcher knife

"Feast"

wiikonge – (vai) give a feast

waabooz – (na) snowshoe hair

banajaanh – (na) baby bird

> in this story there are no more catastrophes only animals that track their lives through the snow.

maanadikoshens – (na) goat

bezhigwan – (vi) be one, be the only one

bimikawaan – (ni) footprint, track

"Grammar"

zhiishiib – (na) duck

wiidige – (vai) marry, be married

doodooshaaboo – (ni) milk

gookoosh – (na) pig

ninaabem – (nad) my husband

"Hysteria"

gwiingwa'aage – (na) wolverine

giiwanaadizi – (na) be crazy, be insane ~~hunger for other~~
to remain

"Idiom"

awaakan – (na) domestic animal, slave

wiindigoo – (na) wiindigoo: winter cannibal monster

maji-manidoo – (na) evil manitou, devil

gizhaadigewinini – (na) game warden

abinoojiinyag – (na pl) children

wiisaaakodewininiwag – (na pl) people of mixed ancestry

manitou is spirit   medicine   even bad spirits are not always evil
sometime they are   just playing tricks on you   helping you
learn this lesson you were meant to learn

"Jaaga'e"

jaaga'e – (vai) use up all of the ammunition

akiwenzii – (na) old man

mizise – (na) turkey

nimishoo – (nad) grandpa

waagikomaaan – (ni) crooked knife

"Kindergarten"

Fig. 34.—Mink. (Drawn by Ernest S. Thompson.)
Latreola vison energumenos (Bangs). Pacific Mink.
Common along the streams at Sisson, where R. T. Fisher caught two,
one on Cold Creek, the other on the upper Sacramento River.
21753—No. 16——14

minks are prized for their fur. once hunted, they are now farmed and slaughtered.

zhaangweshi – (na) mink

"Lament"

gichi-mookomaan – (na) white person, american (ni) butcher knife

ozhaawashko – (pv4) blue, green

bebezhigooganzhii – (na) horse

> to name one thing by its association with another

"Mohawk"

miigaadiwin – (ni) battle, war

"Nishkoonzh"

nishkoonzh – (nid) my snout

nishiime – (nad) my younger sibling

nishiwe – (vai) kill people

"Optics"

omoodayaabik – (ni) bottle

"Possess"

mamigaade – (vii) be taken, be picked up

"Quell"

maanishtaanish – (na) sheep

"Recusant"

ojibweg – (na pl) Ojibwe

jiibaakwewakik – (na) cooking pot, pan

jiibay – (na) ghost, spirit

gichi-mookomaanag – (na pl) white people

"Scythe : Giishkizhigan"

bimaaji'aad – (vta prt) save the life of

giishkizhigan – (ni) scyth

"Totem"

indooodem doodam   do something   my clan

"Uvula"

zhawimin – (ni) grape

zhawenjige – (vai) be merciful

"Varmint"

adik – (na) caribou, reindeer

miigaadiwin – (ni) battle, war

gichi-mookomaanag – (na pl) white people

anishinaabe-bimaadizi – (vai) live the Indian way

zhagashkaandawe – (na) flying squirrel

"Wiikwaji'o"

wiikwam – (vta) suck on, draw on

wiikwajitoon – (vai) try to do, try to get free of ~~to act out of~~
   ~~shame or grief~~

wiikwaji'o – (vai) try to get free

gichi-mookomaan – (na) ~~white person, american~~ (ni) butcher knife

aniibiishaabookewininiiwi – (na) Chinese

"Xylem"

miigwan – (na) feather

anishinaabeg – (na pl) people, Indians, Ojibwe

wanagek – (na) bark

"Ya'aw : Yo'o"

ya'aw – (pr) that

yo'o – (pr) this

"Ziiginigewigamig"

ziiginigewigamig – (ni) tavern, bar

akiwenziiyag – (na pl) old men

Ritual and access. At the turn of the 20th century, it was permissible in Minnesota to license one saloon per 500 persons. In San Francisco in the 1950s, the ration was set at one per 2,000. A half a century later, in the Tenderloin—one of San Francisco's densest and poorest districts—the ratio is one to 186.

Aja Couchois Duncan is a Bay Area educator, writer and coach of Ojibwe, French and Scottish descent. Her writing has been anthologized in *Biting the Error: Writers Explore Narrative* (Coach House Press), *Bay Poetics* (Faux Press) and *Love Shook My Heart 2* (Alyson Press). Her most recent chapbook, *Nomenclature, Miigaadiwin, a Forked Tongue* was published by CC Marimbo press. A fictional writer of non-fiction, she has published essays in the *North American Review* and *Chain*. In 2005, she was a recipient of the Marin Arts Council Award Grant for Literary Arts, and, in 2013, she received a James D. Phelan Literary Award. She holds an MFA in Creative Writing from San Francisco State University and a variety of other degrees and credentials to certify her as human. Great Spirit knew it all along.

Author illustration by Goose Gutierrez, Bay Area animator, gusgutierrez.com